Tyranny of Hope

Pamela Borawski

illustrated by baroque-fables.deviantart.com

To my family, who loved me even through the
darkest years in which these poems were born.

illustration by Pamela Borawski
Hope flutters free...

What readers have said about Pamela's poetry:

"You still blow me away with your style. Such rhythm and composure and that vocabulary; it sings. You tell vivid stories in such short comprehensible stanzas, It's nice." – elzora.deviantart.com

"...I like your style. Certainly much more readable than most poetry I've seen." – nickmandler.deviantart.com

"Your poetry is never anything other than heartfelt. I appreciate the genuine thought you put into each one of your poems!" "You have put into words what most people can only feel! Expressing it can be oh too hard for so many...as always, your soul ... shines through." – sya.deviantart.com

"I admire your consistent ability to show not only the dark side of optimism's standbys, like hope, but more than that, you show that these things can crush a person just as easily, if not more so, than the blatant despair itself." – softlybeatensoul.deviantart.com

"...as always, your imagery startles me in its lucidity." "There are no errors in this, just truth. Oddly melancholy, yet hopeful in some way I can't comprehend...it's beautiful." – goji.deviantart.com

"I like your descriptions and the eloquence with which you always paint your pictures." – sanguinesolitude.deviantart.com

"Another applause worthy piece.. keep this up and I might have to put down the pen in defeat." – thedarkdevice00.deviantart.com

"The visualization in [that poem] was amazingly well done. I could really feel what you were saying, I can relate to that feeling, reaching for that hand that was not there... alone." – deadeyes2021.deviantart.com

"Your words just make little nests inside me and blossom into beauty." – cudlpnk.deviantart.com

"You've done a nice job in blending eloquent wordings with subtle meanings to create a rather expressive piece." – wombatman5042.deviantart.com

"I love the use of figurative language, you have the talent to make the piece come alive for the reader." "For lack of a better metaphor, it's as though you can capture emotions in a jar and keep them perfectly preserved. ...you capture so much emotion with such simplicity that you truly follow what I believe to be the real purpose of poetry." – winged-cavalier.deviantart.com

"You really illustrate the sorrow you're feeling well." – pokes.deviantart.com

"Seems to be talking of something so sad...yet, you make it sound as if it weren't!" – classique.deviantart.com

"Wow. I love this! You just took that big bunch of mush in my head and turned it into poetry." – dead-poet.deviantart.com

"Your vocabulary is tremendously wonderful and very complex. This is exactly what poetry is- words chosen to amplify and emphasize exactly what you are trying to convey in this poem, this single thought." – n03113.deviantart.com

"You've said here what I've always wanted to scream to the world, but was taught not to by society. Thank you." – softlybeatensoul.deviantart.com

Acknowledgements

A special thanks to my mother Alley; without her help this project would not exist. She tirelessly spent countless hours assisting me in revision and editing.

Congratulations to Simon Falk for winning the cover art contest. Thank you for entering and allowing me to use your wonderful work of art for the cover of this book of poetry. To see more of Simon's work, check out beautywithanedge.deviantart.com.

Also a big thank you to all the talented artists at deviantart.com that have given me permission to use their art. Many of them took time to illustrate my poems with new work. I really appreciate their creativity and efforts. Please visit their galleries.

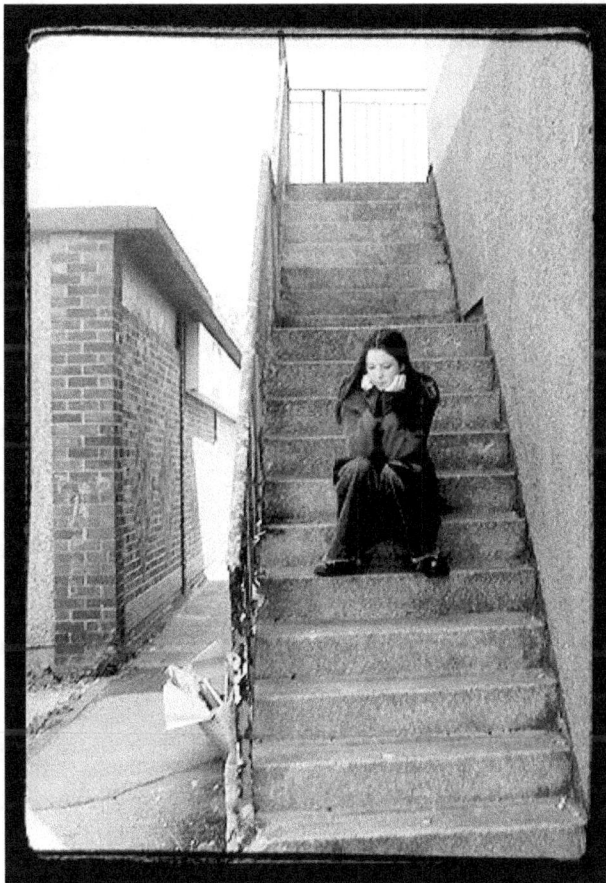

illustration by kitsch-object.deviantart.com

Table of Contents

A Note to the Reader

There is no doubt that this collection of poetry is dark, even morbid at times. I believe everyone goes through rough times in their life, some worse than others. These poems were brought to life in my darkest times; they are my autobiography. They came to fruition when the darkness was reaching for me, clutching at me with its icy claws and trying to sink me beneath a mire of despondency and depression. Hitting rock bottom hurts, not only physically but emotionally and spiritually too. These poems are a glimpse into the soul of a person who has lost everything, including hope. For hope is a tyrant, an oppressive power that we all reach for day after day, just so we can slide out of bed each morning. Hope bears down on us in our darkest hours, trying to make you see a light at the end of the filthy tunnel. We strive for hope, it's our life's work. Yet there is a tyranny of hope, a wonder of whether it can truly be accomplished. The darkness fights hard against hope, it wants you to look down instead of up, to stay shackled instead of gain freedom. It wants you to desire death instead of life, for life has lost its joy and only in death will we be truly free from its tyranny.

Perhaps one of these poems will touch your heart. If so, then I have accomplished my goal. My goal is that when you read these very personal miniature life-stories, you will find compassion in your heart for those whose companion is the dark and dreary. Maybe you will find a poem that allows you to express how you feel, and it gives you understanding of your own emotions. I like to think of these poems as little word pictures that gives you a peek into a darkened soul. A soul who has been forgotten, lost, and kicked to the curb. I ask you to open your heart and mind to what the myriad of words within might teach you. I believe that the darkness causes us to appreciate the light even more, for without darkness the light does not shine as brightly.

Pamela Borawski – widdendreams@gmail.com
www.pamelaski.deviantart.com

Tyranny of Hope

There is a tyranny of hope
which attaches itself
to an unspoiled life.

Shattered.
Perhaps next time?
Hope is this thing with feathers
that takes chunks from our flesh,
then flaps away with but a
mellowing laugh left in its wake.

Battered.
It won't happen again.
Slammed against the cold wall of reality,
it makes you open your eyes
to the foolishness of thinking
tomorrow will be a better day.

Tattered.
Where's the bright side?
Torn and tormented yet still
pressing onwards to a dream so real,
but like a mirage which never
quite seems to be attainable.

illustration by Regan Henley ~ popcorn-cob.deviantart.com

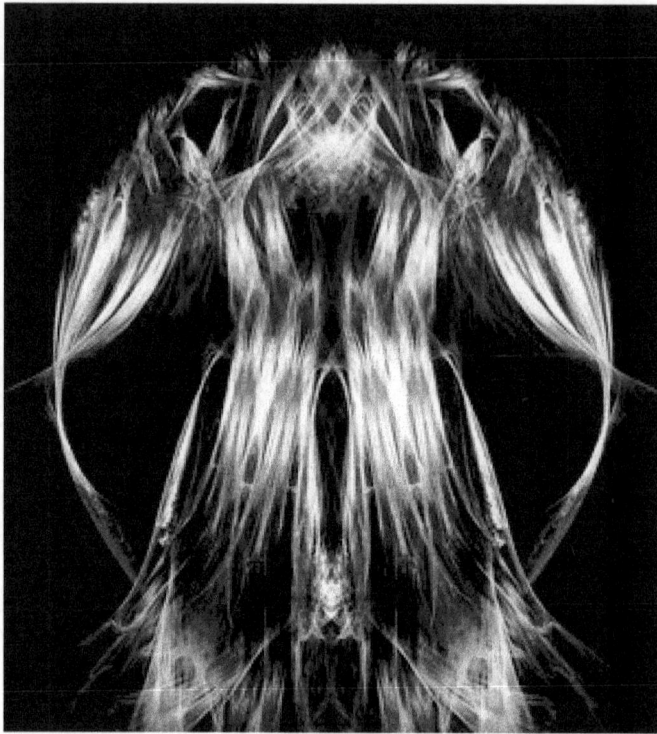

illustration by sya.deviantart.com

Widdendreams

Flickering black to white,
I dwell in a widdendream
of stark opportunity.
Lost in a sea supreme
of suppositions
I never quite fulfill;
I walk a razor's edge
in this surreality,
leaving bloody footprints
in my wake.

This winding dream
slices through my vernacular
leaving my tongue bleeding.
A widening dreamscape
painted for posterity;
showcasing a syntax
of sharpened widdendreams.

Soulscape

In the barren vastness of my soul,
my heart lies forgotten and abused.
The thick, gray atmosphere pervades,
only broken by the trickling tears
that bathed the mound of red flesh,
purifying its duress with a sighing thump.

Every now and then, a figure approaches;
dirty and exhausted from the grueling journey.
Once the heart is reached, tenderly it's lifted.
Cradled and caressed with empathic tears,
the slippery, delicate mass is held close
and for a short time the beat is steady.

My soul is a lonely place, so cold.
My heart is a slippery bastard, fragile.
As it is held so close, grip is lost,
and down with a thud into the fog
of even greater pain and loneliness.
When the thick surroundings clear, it is all alone.

The tears that follow burrow a river of distrust
through the monotony of my soulscape.

illustration by shukugumo.deviantart.com

13

The Enemy

Sanctioned by the enemy
to pull down the bulwarks within.
Crumbling, falling, the foundation failed.

Lying in the mire of my own complacency.
Drowning in the depths of my own blindness.

Pale and frail, the gaunt hand lifts...
for a light flickered. A strong hand appeared.

In vain.

The thick fog encompasses me again,
and heavy lids close as hope flies away
on its many feathered wings.

"Whom shall I cry out to?" it says.

Cry out? Never!
Not even a whimper.
I'll live through the deepening darkness
with few to guide me.

If only...

NO! Those words are taboo!

I am this island.
I am this craggy precipice.

Courted by the enemy,
caressed by the light;
abandoned by the fellowship,
forgotten once out of sight.

Tropical Depression

Get out the umbrella,
there's a rainstorm brewing beneath my skin.
Boiling and bubbling over, threatening dark clouds
move across the horizon of my life
in a never ending line of unhappiness.

The lightning strikes from the heavens,
tarnishing this cold existence called life.
The floodwaters rise within, drowning out all
cries for help that come from the soul
that lies buried in the depths of dependence.

It's monsoon weather beneath my skin,
my stomach churns and turns, and twists in a knot.
The very foundation is shaken to the core
by the storm that rages on endlessly,
and seems to have no end in sight.

And finally, the floodwaters rise above the line
and overflow their boundaries, sending salty
streams of despair across my pale countenance.
But quickly, the waters recede just enough where they
are held in check, and the facade is raised once again.

illustration by Pamela Borawski ~ druideye.deviantart.com

15

Freedom

This fragile shell enfolds who I really am.

I beg for release.
I scream, I claw, I cry.

Beating bloody hands upon the inner flesh of my existence.

Light? Light!

Five lines of light as a hand moves down,
but quickly, too quickly, this cloak of flesh runs aground.

Stumbling back into the darkness,
insanity seems a release.
Lucid thoughts, unresponsive flesh,
makes misery compound.

A prisoner of my very flesh and blood!
My cell will soon weaken,
and I'll be free -

Sweet Freedom.

illustration by Regan Henley ~ popcorn-cob.deviantart.com

illustration by Amir Elizur ~ darklylit.deviantart.com

Eidolon of Longing

What is this feeling that threatens to overtake,
that whispers in my ear at night,
and saunters around the gate?
This emotional upheaval unknown by most
falls short of heaven's blessings,
yet there is hell to pay.

The mortal bonds of flesh and blood
beg for release from bondage.
Yet I must ask myself again
Is this a risk I am willing to take?

This longing, this obsession, this thrilling sensation,
is it the truth or yet another lie?
And again I am held by patience.
Frightening, exciting, my senses overwhelmed.
Could there be hope within my soul
or is dire emptiness only to be found?

The wall is strong, fortified
through many, many years.
Is there a crack? A longing crack,
a crumble in the foundation?
Or is that a mere illusion.
forced upon by seclusion?

Apparently not.

Someone Else

Leather and gold chains
around my heart, mind and soul.
Beaten and bruised because
that's what a leader should do.

He spoke of a Light.
I know it's not right.

Living sacrifice. Take me, use me;
this was my battle cry.
Alone surpassing miles upon miles,
giving it all for the Crown.

He spoke of a Way.
And prostrate I lay.

Words entwined, ingrained...
I followed the program.
The dogma was deep in my heart,
something I lived my life by.

He spoke of a Truth.
Now I'm cold and aloof.

Innocence was torn from my arms.
Violently ripped from my hands.
Then doubt buried in my heart,
I rose with a cynical taint.

He spoke of a Joy.
I was his childhood Toy.

I always did all I was told,
I walked the narrow path.
The sorrows rained down heavily.
I ran and disappeared into the "secular" world.

He spoke of New Life.
It cut me like a knife.

Someone else so many years,
who could I please?
There was no one, not even myself,
wearing the skin of piety.

He spoke of a Day.
I've gone another way.

I wonder if a time will come
when I can be who I am.
When I can speak with passion,
without hearing the voice of death.

He spoke in my ear...
No longer do I hear.

illustration by plif.deviantart.com

Quietus

Collapsing tenuous membrane.
Dry and cracked taut skin opens,
gasping soundlessly, arms flail.
Nostrils flare, begging for breath.

The forest hidden behind the
striated gate begins to wither.
The softest of whistles like a
summer's breeze whispering
pierces the engulfing air.

Struck by your own first knight.
Stabbed in the back, perforation.
The hole small, so insignificant,
yet a cogent force, quietus.

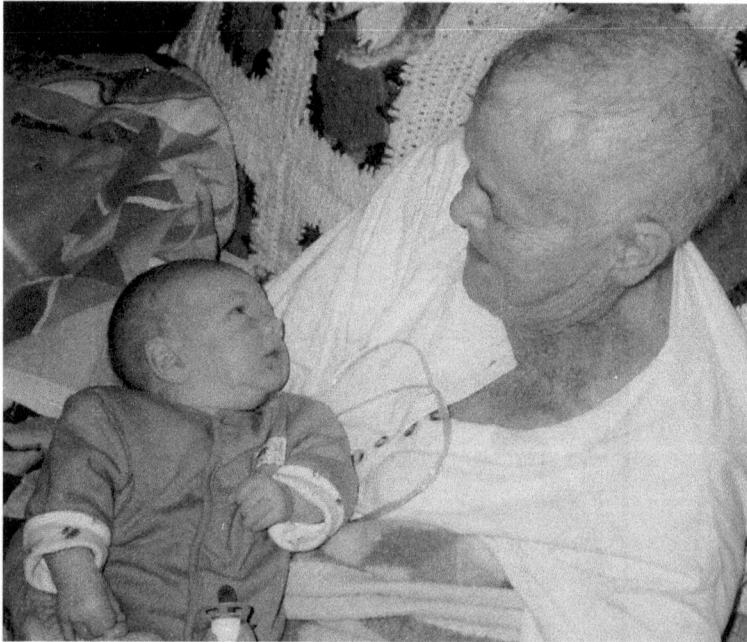

illustration by Pamela Borawski ~ druideye.deviantart.com
*My grandmother the day before she died with my oldest son.
She had cancer and a collapsed lung.*

illustration by frozen-scumbag.deviantart.com

Indifference

Boiling beneath the skin of a complacent religiosity,
hollow cries echo within the empty,
lifeless walls of your own doing.
Brick after brick encompassing mind and soul,
securing them from contact with the outside.
Fruitless attempts to scale the slippery walls,
while above the eyes watch and take no heed.
Are you even there?
Do you even care?

It eats you from within, devouring at the cellular level,
leaving an empty shell and a
rotted, stinking mess between the ears.
Warfare rages between light and dark or so we were taught.
What really happens in the realms of the unseen?
Are Michael and the Beautiful One taking tea?
The world as we know it shimmers and fades from reality.
Are you even there?
Do you even care?

Don't Mention It

I am called "Dark".
I am pinned "Dangerous".
But do you really know me?

You play at friendship.
Your facade is chipping'
Soon you'll be as dirty as me.

White washed sepulchers.
Hypocrites and whores.
That's what you all are to me.

Climb back into your dirty hole,
and don't let my name slip from
your sweetly sour tongue again!

illustration by Pamela Borawski ~ druideye.deviantart.com

Echoes of Pain

Pain
Echoes in my soul.
Filters through my mind.
Surging
forward in my veins
until I scream in release.
Completed,
until another day.

Mom Opens the Door

Sorrow.
A youth falls, lost
in mists of sweat and blood.
Cold and alone, two voices call,
"Come home."

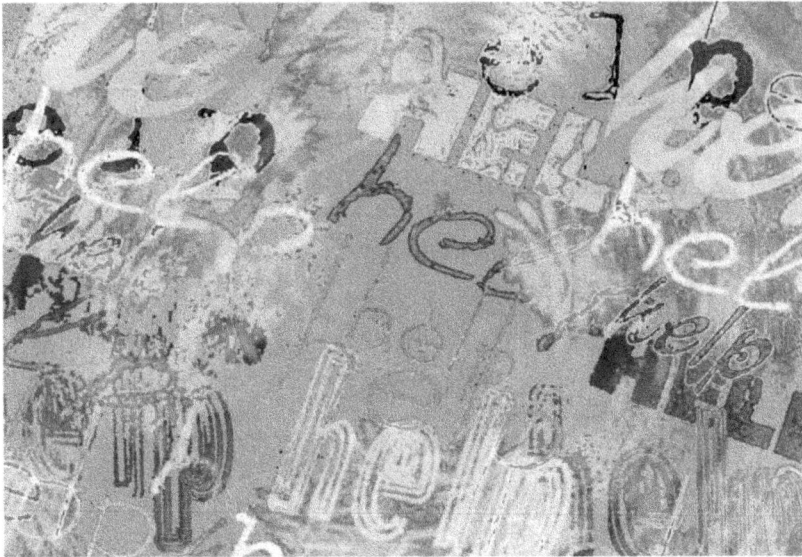

illustration by majik721.deviantart.com

Dark Seven

Rings of ebony, the shadow watcher
crouches amidst the falling rain of woe.
Foreboding mists hang heavy in the streets,
crafty creatures long forgotten emerge.

"More!" the haughty laugh of one soaring high,
the self-imposed pedestal tottering with each breath.

"More!" comes the cry of the penny-pincher,
amassed wealth filthy with the stench of deceit.

"More!" the raspy cry of bodies entwined,
sweat drenched and slippery with immorality.

"More!" as bite after bite is shoveled to satiate,
though never enough, bloated with excess.

"More!" gazing across at the neighbors wares,
in the midst of abundance, pining for exchange.

"More!" as a fist pummels a loved one's face,
wrathful fire lit, only quenched by abuse.

"More," comes the sleepy voice as the alarm rings,
time passes, yet nothing is done, fettered with avoidance.

The attack is made, vile beasts of shadows
burrowing their way unannounced into the soul.
Slime-ridden feet take root and blossom
into a protruding flower of diablerie.

7

illustration by Andrea Schmoll ~ greenfaery.deviantart.com

Noon Tea and Poetry

Pacify the stony ground
with ill-iterated tea.
Dripping of parsimonious
anger and liberty.

Crucify the only one
that ever gave you hope.
Bury them beneath a mound
of julienned jokes.

Dredge them up to play again,
you sapient lying bastard.
I should have known my heart was stone
and made my judgment faster.

Next Contestant, Please

Dilly-dally! Heidi-ho!
Life is like a sick game show.
First your name is called to the front,
then your ass is given the punt.
Finally, at the end of the round,
your broken body is shoved in the ground.

illustration by Pamela Borawski ~ druideye.deviantart.com

Contrition

Dejected; utterly, incredibly alone.

The prostration of my soul
has caused my eyes to peer down.
Is this contrition the cause
of the self-loathing, or the effect?

Tormented; completely, overwhelmingly in pain.

Every synapse in my flesh
brings agony as I move.
My sedulous pursuit to
assuage hurt is devoid of merit.

Rejected; undeniably, simply shut out.

illustration by devilevn.deviantart.com

Ode to Hypocrisy

Abased; the sycophantic dilemma
brings me to my knees...
bowing before one so strong
that all he is seems weak.

Clothed so pretty in garments of culture,
and tongue so laced with venom.
You spout off the verses that hold you so tight,
but do you really believe them?

Humility is a guise for the broken,
inside you're a demonic prude.
Though such things you'd never stoop to,
wear your self-righteous dissimilitude.

The tyrannical blustering wind you produce,
would melt the staunchest of pillars.
How about taking care of that log in your eye,
before you make note of my splinter.

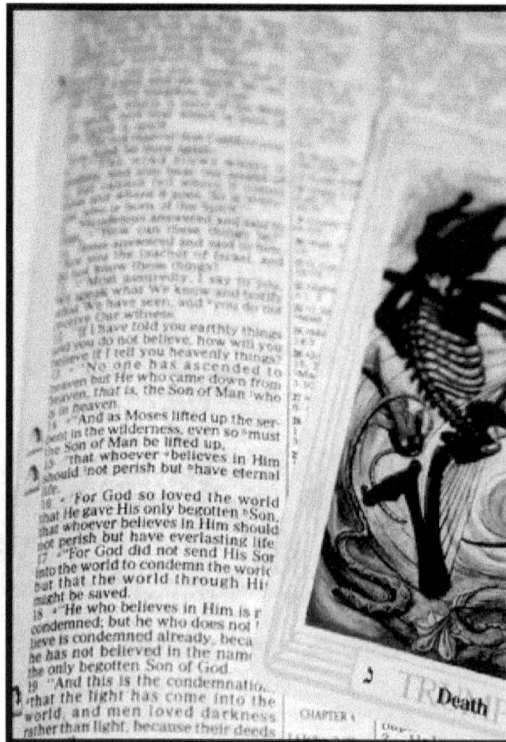

illustration by Pamela Borawski ~ druideye.deviantart.com

Precious Treasures

My burial shroud is pink silk,
with three pearly buttons down the front.
I pulled it on and stared in the mirror.
Brushed my hair, sobriety unseen.

Grey wooden planks scream my approach.
I open the door, I stand at the threshold.
Three steps to freedom, short walk to doom;
I walked the path of destruction,
but something caught my eye.

Late Sunday night, the moon so high,
it lit the yard and there it was...
A lost trinket from a sunny day.
A quarter hid in the short grass.

I tried to walk beside it,
this was for the best.
This was for their best.

Yet the silver stayed in my vision.
Over I bent to pick up the coin in my hand.
I raised my fist to throw it...
but couldn't.

My soul screamed for release,
but my heart clung to its covering.
Tears fell as I ran barefoot in pain,
sliced by the road.

I stopped and turned around.
My house was lit up by the lights,
my son's precious treasure in hand.

A failure; I can't even end my life.
Now I sit penning this tale,
wondering if there will be another.

Toxicological Wasteland

My tears cannot assuage
the pain of my pierced heart.
The poison of deceit
has tainted my vision.
The blurry lines of fate
entangle and choke.

What life I had,
in happy dread,
has fallen fallow.

Like clay, so easily swayed,
molded into a lovely thing.
Pure worship to my creator,
until the fist comes
slamming down, flattening out,
crushing its very being.

Scarred and marred,
ripped into by a forked tongue
like the serpent of old.
Stumbling into the void,
of manipulated creation.

illustration by Pamela Borawski ~ druideye.deviantart.com

The Shackles of Freedom

What repercussions stain these sheets,
as I lay within encircled flesh?
Melting into one being,
when youth has yet to flourish.

Promises that will never be kept;
A seed planted willingly yet unknowingly
Then faded into shadows,
only a surname left in the wake.

What sorrows come from such delight;
the price of freedom is unbearable.
Yet bear it, I will have to do;
jealous descent into maturity.

Never again will I be one.

Purity was traded for responsibility.
My loss will now be a gain,
and the freedom I wanted so desperately
has become bonds holding me tight--
as I play house in shackles.

illustration by Pamela Borawski ~ druideye.deviantart.com

clipart from gothic-pictures.net

The Death Match

I found myself too busy
and didn't give Death his due.
So Death paid me a visit,
and such a fuss did ensue.

He asked why I didn't meet him,
as I promised that I would.
I stuttered and mumbled and stammered,
and shrugged as before him I stood.

He didn't quite like my silence.
Eyes darkened as he stared.
Bony, gaunt hands tapped together,
if only I'd been prepared.

Now Death's no respecter of persons.
Hell, he took both my Uncle and Gram.
Now he stands here to claim me,
seems my hourglass is all out of sand.

Each day that I fight against him,
I find I grow weaker still.
What a struggle it is to resist him.
One day I will falter...but 'til...

'Til that day overpowers me,
'til my life draws to a close,
'til my eyes shut forever,
I fight for the sake of my soul.

Sunday's Child

I am a cookie cutter Christian.
I wear my faith on my chest,
but beneath the fabric that taunts the Savior
beats a heart anything but blessed.

My smile is painted across me.
God always wants joy on our face.
It matters not what's inside you,
there's no defeat, in the holy race.

I go to church when the doors open,
and I know all the right words to say.
I can cut someone right down to the quick,
with what I learned from last Sunday.

All my sins are forgiven.
Yet there are sins I don't know.
Sins of submission and sins of omission,
but all of these sins God foreknows.

But our pastor always enlightens us,
of "new" no-no's that appear in our world.
Seems this week the color is pink...
the transgressions of life are unfurled.

Or no... I meant a rainbow,
that's "gay" in satan-speak.
Heaven forbid we associate with such;
the dark, the sickening, the weak.

All the toys are after our children.
I'll picket with all my friends.
Lord have mercy on our souls;
even Saturday cartoons offend.

I'll sing "when we all get to heaven,"
and turn away from the bum in my path;
'cause he smells like old whiskey,
and he must be under God's wrath.

'Cause any brethren that hurts
just has some sin in their life.
If only they'd repent; turn a new leaf,
they'd no longer have sickness or strife.

I am a faithful disciple,
a New Testament in my backpack.
I'll quote full passages to you;
don't expect me to take feedback.

When I eat out at a restaurant,
a tract is left instead of a tip.
I know that my precious Savior
will reward me for honest saint ship.

Look at me all you heathens,
my life is so good; best repent!
I keep all my problems hidden,
and pray for the day of ascent.

Too much self, they say, is a burden;
we pray, "die to self" every day.
I am a cookie cutter Christian,
I'll fit in when I cut "me" away.

illustration by maguxmagu.deviantart.com

Purgatory of Feelings

I cannot tell lies,
nor can I tell the truth.
A purgatory of feelings,
that way-lays the heart.

Seduced by true love;
fallen into quagmire.
An elegantly laid trap
whose secrets ensnare.

I was an easy prey,
and now I am devoured.

illustration by frozen-scumbag.deviantart.com

Stifling

Arbitrary lie,
that I must deny.
You're wrong.

See, I won't comply,
need not even try.
So long.

Holding my reply,
I'm gone, now goodbye.
Be strong.

Illustration by psychobubble.deviantart.com

Psycho Semantic

There are children that
giggle and laugh
outside my bathroom window.

Two men that play chess
every single night
at my dining room table.

A couple that fights,
a baby that cries,
and someone who taps
on the panes of glass.

They don't seem to mind
my presence at all,
catching a glimpse from
the corner of my eye.

I wasn't too lonely,
I had all these friends,
but apparently-
that wasn't healthy.

In my tiny, stark room
where they put me away,
visitors were not made welcome.

Ashamed to admit that I miss
the men playing chess, and
singing to the crying baby.

illustration by kingsnake2.deviantart.com

Dark

Tendrils of ebon
twist their strands
around my dying soul.

Tainted by shadows,
though there is no grey.

Hidden in obscurity,
my darkest intentions
are caressed by
svelte silken sighs.

The Thread

Delicate, the balance
of mind and soul.
Surreptitiously it creeps
between the threads
of sanity-
writhing on the border;
falling, and hanging on
like butterfly wings
caught in a tornado.

illustration by Pamela Borawski ~ druideye.deviantart.com

illustration by S.R. Greenfield ~ deadgods.deviantart.com

Death's Lover

Death calls to me in the dark of the night.
His cool, rank breath caresses me.
The touch of bone slides up my thigh.
I can't help but utter a slow, soft sigh.

His promises are sounding better and better.
Icy cold lips press against my flesh.
He says he'll be the best lover I ever had.
He says I'll never cry, I'll never be sad.

He tugs relentlessly at my garments of flesh.
He'll be my friend, he'll rescue me.
All the cares of this world will fade.
He says he keeps every promise he made.

Such a touch, such a sweet respite.
He offers to carry me away from here.
He'll be my best lover, he'll be my friend,
all I have to say is "I want it to end..."

His panting in my ear gives me chills.
If I truly loved him I'd give in.
If I'd let him consummate his love,
together as one we'd rise above.

illustration by baroque-fables.deviantart.com

My Dying Flower

My dying flower
droops in a vase.
The petals flutter
one by one
to the floor.

As death claims its very scent,
my dying flower sinks slowly.
Even a sympathetic drink
seems unattainable,
leaving it brittle and dry.

Plucked up and crumbled,
my dying flower
is tossed away
for her beauty
is spent.

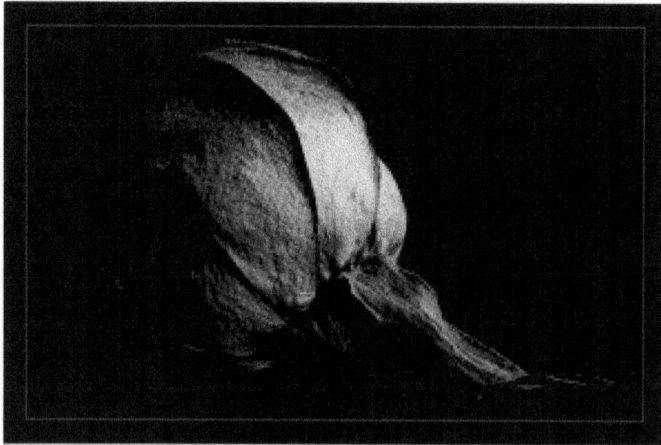

illustrated by Daniel Devlicharov ~ digitaldreamz666.deviantart.com

illustration by blue-eyed-snidget.deviantart.com

Hope Deferred

Hope has abrogated,
in its place lies despair.
Bitter vines clench my heart.
The wounds are beyond repair.

The buoyancy of my youth
has sprung a leak.
I'm drowning in despondency,
salty tears are what I drink.

Some say it only is deferred-
but hope deferred others say...
is like a raisin in the sun
shriveled and dried where it lay.

Perhaps hope's like a hot air balloon.
You rise above it all.
Someone's shooting at me now.
Take cover! Down I fall...

Cracked Vessel

You labeled me for destruction.
I was chosen for humiliation.
A tender, young vessel.

So much like a god you were;
a god in man's clothing.
A demon in god's visage.
Heinous were your acts.
You took pride in screwing with our brains.
Now we're all little lost sheep.

Like lambs to the slaughter,
your hands led us.
In the guise of "just good fun",
your hands were full of lust.

Were your thoughts as pious as your words?
Or were your thoughts diabolical in nature?

Taking the sweet fruit of the young,
squeezing out our innocence
without even a passing word.

Tormented, frightened, we thought we'd done wrong.
I'm sure some of us still do...
Not me, you bastard, not me at all!
YOU were the sinner! YOU were the monster!

Do your secret longings bother you?
Your lust for that which you cannot have?

I hope your life is twice the hell that mine is.
Fuck you, and keep your hands to yourself.

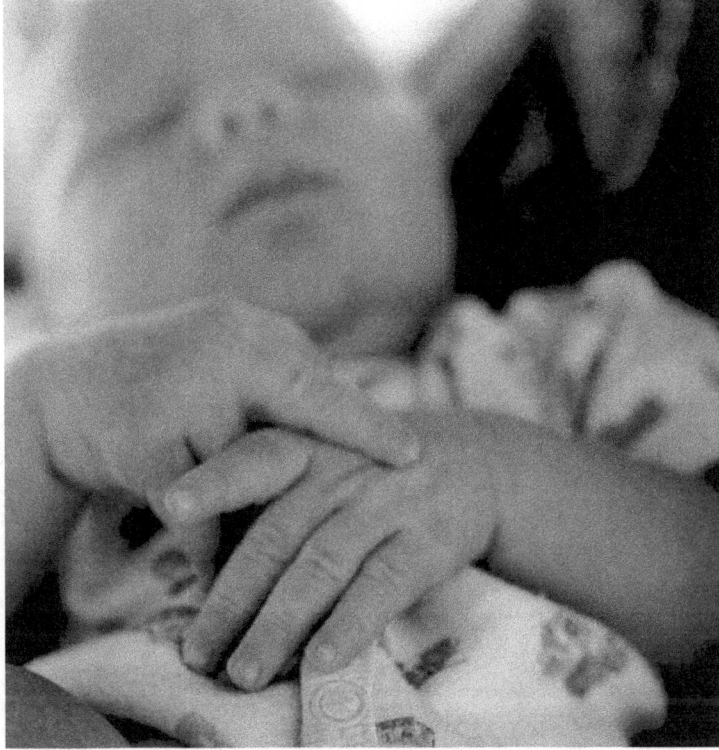

illustration by Pamela Borawski ~ druideye.deviantart.com

Hymn of the Diaboli

Malicious in intent.
Contemptibly content.
Brother of my blood.
Lover of my needs.
Your blood fulfills
my deepest desires.
My blood for you pleads.
I worship your vicious attack.
I long for the demon inside me.
I'll forcefully take your seed.
You'll lovingly make me bleed.
And within the cold darkness
I'll claim you as my own.

illustration by h-agnostic.deviantart.com

Myrage

My anger has been a long time coming.
I've held it in so long.
But now it's out, you'd better take cover,
my inner rage grows strong.

I stand here alone and take a good look,
like a mirage life floats around me.
Hopes and Dreams, I pant for them;
stumbling closer I will be free.

The mirage of my life once I arrived,
became shifting sand all around.
And Hopes and Dreams float away,
now My Rage has pulled me down.

Damn you! Throwing sand in my eyes...
as towards the mirage I crawl.
I rub my eyes, my vision blurs,
now, nothing's here at all!

illustration by psychobubble.deviantart.com

The Circus Life

Life is a bucket of manure
teetering on the end of a
clown's high wire act.

The lions roar in rage,
while the audience laughs
in magnanimous support.

The jeers only make the clown
move faster along the razor-sharp
wire of our destiny.

Then, oops!

Amidst an applause sign lit up,
and the crowd going wild,
an elephant tramples and stomps
through the spilled manure
of what was once held so dear.

illustration by Pamela Borawski ~ druideye.deviantart.com

Dilapidated

Empty as the vacant house
that sits on Swygert Road.

That house always intrigued me.
Sitting there in the woods,
covered in kudzu and honeysuckle vines:
its porch sagging, tin roof caved in.

If walls could talk...
If ghosts walked its floorboards...
I'm sure the stories would be like my life.

Some happy, some sad.
Tragedy as its sons and daughters
were buried one by one.
Now abandoned, forgotten, left to rot alone.

Like my soul.

illustration by Pamela Borawski ~ druideye.deviantart.com

In Memory of Uncle Bebo

Consequential Why?

I pleaded with the "Almighty One",
just make it go away.
Just cleanse his soul, cleanse his life
and please God let him stay.

And all my pleas fell on deaf ears,
upon a mound I stood.
The sky above, the sand beneath,
his body enclosed in wood.

The tears fell down and hit the dirt,
a song was sung aloud.
A cry was heard, a shout to him,
I always made him proud.

And all I asked, one simple word,
spoken from the heart.
This little word emptied my life,
as I saw his soul depart.

Why?

Tell me why?
Will you tell me why?
Don't I deserve to know why?

Why did he have to go?
Why did you have such a plan?
Why did you break my heart?
I just can't understand.

He was ill, this I know,
but he didn't have to be.
You could have healed his body
like so many through history.

But no...
You said no...
I heard you say no...
You just *had* to say no...

Do you hate me this much
that you would take from me,
the very one that filled my life
with love, ignoring my plea?

I'm mad at you, "Almighty One",
where was your might today?
When your own dear child
begged for him to stay?

Own dear child, such a joke,
I guess it was my fate,
that my life would be destroyed
by one I've come to hate.

The hurt within is much to bear,
I can barely say his name
this loss I feel, this emptiness,
I'll never be the same.

illustration by Regina Day ~ dead-poet.deviantart.com

She's Gone

A pervading fear entered the house,
moving through the rooms
until the weak was seen.
He gave a nod, and a light snort,
and reaped her soul as well.

There I lay in the other room,
thinking I was here on vacation,
but gloom and darkness
pierced the day,
as did the sun on the horizon.

A scream roared through
the house that morn,
a scream that broke my sleep.
The words struck my heart
like a sharpened blade.

"She's gone! She's gone!"

I jumped up, and into her room I ran,
kneeling by the bed.
On her side, in quiet sleep,
her soul communed with others long dead.
I could not touch her, I could only stare,
then shuffle through the house.

The men, they came,
and wrapped her up,
and carted her away,
I could only stand and stare,
shocked at the events of this day.
Little one at my breast,
tears kissed his cheek,
for he wouldn't know her.

I had a wound, gashed wide by death,
two years before that day.
And on this tumultuous day of grief,
that gaping wound was twisted open again,
without mercy, a settling sense of urgency
and emptiness filled my life.

Again I stood on a mound of sand,
staring at her flowers.
A song was sung in quietness,
though I cried out within to the heavens.

That same question I had asked before,
so simple in its repetition,
but it found a home dripping from my lips,
one I still have no answer...

"Why?"

In Memory of Marie

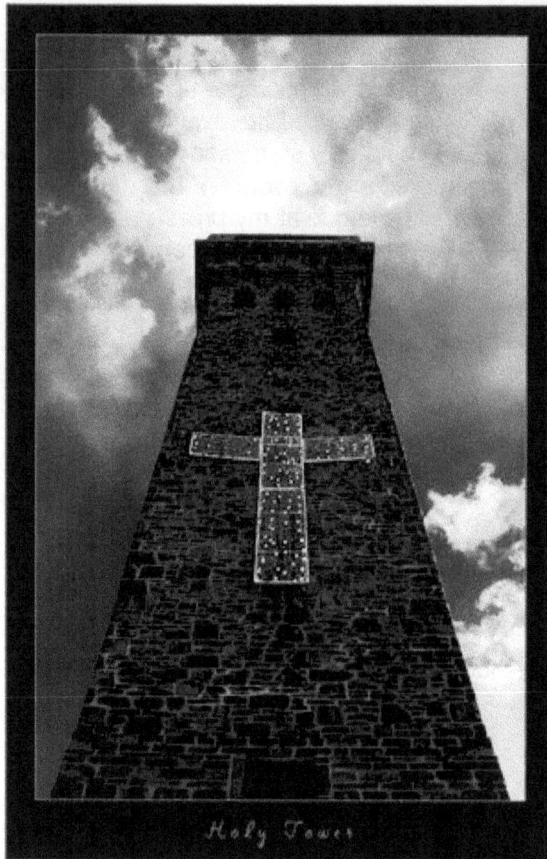

illustration by Nita Hein ~ lobsterclaws.deviantart.com

Renewed Vision

I've done all you asked,
and even a little more.
I've denied my own self
to be someone you adored.

It was never enough,
more was always asked.
I lost myself along the way
fulfilling my "god given" task.

No more will I attempt
to be someone for You.
I've decided to be myself,
my vision is renewed.

54

Pomp and Arrogance

You do not know me,
and you never will!
I don't know you,
even better still.

Stand and walk away;
get out of my life.
Stop trying so hard,
I'm not your humble wife.

Marriage is for the birds,
and men can go to hell.
Self-righteous sacrilege...
Oops! I didn't tell.

Put on your Sunday face,
and spout your Sunday words.
It's not Sunday, asshole;
I'll not bow down and serve.

I suppose all who know me
intercede for me.
Your pompous veneration
won't bring ME to MY knees.

Like I told the people
who stopped at my door...
I'm uninterested in ANY god,
goodbye, I want no more!

illustration by dgpc4ever.deviantart.com

illustration by Verena Gremmer ~ vripley.deviantart.com

Cycling Sorrows

Here we go again,
split me open.
Tear my flesh from bone,
flayed emotions,
heart asunder.

Stay in the darkness,
live all alone.
Venture out I ask,
stay true to self?
Put up a façade?

The dark is fright'ning,
scares friends away.
Communicable?
I'm too quiet.
Pretend all's well.

Can't pretend for long,
and the dam breaks.
Like a sweeping torrent.
Drown in sorrow.
Drown in hate.

Out comes the darkness,
deluge of pain.
Left spinning; empty,
so abandoned.
Hurt overwhelms.

Next time try harder,
show nothing wrong.
Feign life is joyous.
Merely pretense.
Seeking a friend.

Cycle continues,
worsens each time.
Wish someone loved me!
Accept who I am.
Darkness and all.

The Cancer of Sorrow

Black as noire
is this corruption
that eats away
the inner flesh
leaving pinkened
and renewed skin
so easily ripped apart
in splitting pain.

illustration by Pamela Borawski ~ druideye.deviantart.com

A Silent Walk

Cold marble under my fingertips,
a forgotten name etched in stone.
Cross over...

Surrounded by trees whose
beauty has been raped by winter.
Cross over...
Join me...

Soft ground, thorns rising from
the moist earth like clawed hands.
Cross over...
Join me...
There's always room for one more.

illustration by Pamela Borawski ~ druideye.deviantart.com

Eternal Night

Desperation of each breath.
Each step weighs heavy upon this life.
Elegantly dying with each gasp,
a fortuitous turn of events.

Sleeping upon the brushed silks.
Dark lashes fluttering no more.
Lips grow pale with a kiss from he
who will carry her to the other side.

The pain has ceased within her flesh.
The battle is over, there is no time.
For time is a thing of the past,
and eternity is what caresses her.

Strolling upon the Elysian Fields.
Basking in the sun of Paradise.
Dancing with the angelic host;
life is over, eternal night begins.

illustration by kingsnake2.deviantart.com

Glory-Bound

She was ready for Glory.

Each passing day,
holding her down.
Her eyes saw further
than what was around.

"I've lived for too long,
everyone else is gone."

She didn't beckon Death,
but willingly crossed that river
when the offer was made.

Prepared for what was to come,
leaving her pain and
memories behind.

illustration by Pamela Borawski ~ druideye.deviantart.com

Paix a Tout Prix

Soul scarred and broken, crushed by my vice,
my battle cry of freedom, "Peace at any price".
Obsessed with a notion that all will be well,
peace at any price is such a hard sell.

Longing to be free, longing to be dead,
this war wages on within my battered head.
The white flag is waving, I know it won't be long,
before I'm taken prisoner, I never was that strong.

The price for peace continues to take its toll,
the price is much more than I bargained for.
But paix a tout prix was the agreement made,
so love, family, health,...this was what I paid.

The war is ever raging, I can hardly bear the fight,
when the end of revolution is still not yet in sight.
My weapons grow dull from their frequent use,
my battle cry is stifled by the traitor's noose.

illustration damphyr.deviantart.com

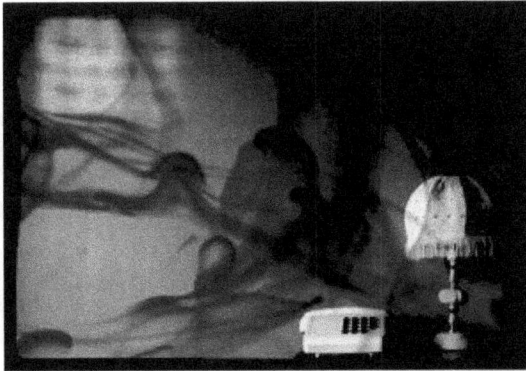

illustration by kitsch-object.deviantart.com

Breathless

I lie to myself with my life's breath,
though I know not why except
I have always done so.

Worthless words wind through
my psyche from ages past
that I struggle to forget.

Lonely feelings grab my heart
at times even in the presence
of my friends and family.

I am silent; I am none.
I am no one; I am shunned.
Who am I, how do I know?
Where am I going, where have I gone?

Quandaries so subtle filter through my brain.
I don't ask aloud, but they're always there.
A scintillating hope that one day
the answers will unfold before my very eyes.

Satisfaction will be mine!
The truth will be known,
even with my dying breath.

illustration by blue-eyed-snidget.deviantart.com

Happily Never After

The broken princess stood on her balcony,
pained eyes closed behind darkened lids.
The softest, saddest of sighs echoed
on the breeze through the garden in winter.
Her breath could easily cloud her vision.
Her whimpers could easily plug her ears.

She whispered into the void of her walls,
"I don't want to be Queen of Nothing,
nor liege of an Empty Land.
I'm tired of following Your footsteps,
I want to know where *I* stand."

Her silent cries were deafening
across the vast expanse.
He heard her cry of desperation
and fell in love at first glance.

He slipped into the garden at midnight,
so silent, so breathless and bold;
garbed entirely in robes of jet black.
Into her chambers he slithered,
and lifted her sickly, pale hand.
She opened her eyes...he was here!

The tender exchange of first kisses,
as his shadowy hands held her close.
He made her promises there in the moonlight.
Sobbing, she lifted her eyes.
"I marry another tomorrow night.
He is King of a land high above us,
with streets of gold and gates of pearl.
My father's mind is made up...
I wish I could leave this world."

"Leave with me...", came his raspy taunt.
"I'll satisfy your every want.
We'll bring them to their knees.
You're the only one you need to please."

She took his hand, to the balcony she stepped;
and like an angel into his arms she leapt.
Her Knight in Shadowy Armour had given her wings.
Never again, no more, would she care for earthly things.

Life's Twists and Turns

Fluttering along the breeze
of supple strands of life's web
until a twitch in the framework
and karma sends us hurtling
like a molten cannonball
through icy space to slam
smack-dab into the weave
of yet another existence.

Alone in a Crowd

Walk a day in my shoes.
Feel what it's like to be me.

This punishment weighs down my soul,
like a never ending storm cloud of tears.
Lonely, hurt, and so very sad.
Is anyone there?
Standing in a crowd, and yet so utterly alone.

My heart cries out,
but I never say a word.
Can't you see the hurt in my eyes?
Can't you hear the hurt in my sighs?
My silent cry for help.

All I wish for is a listening ear,
an understanding heart,
and the security that no matter what I say,
those I love will never go away.

My Eulogy

When garments of flesh are tossed aside,
my soul will shine, my soul will fly.

No longer confined by this mortal coil,
purified of faults and life's hard toil.

The day approaches, I cannot deny;
when cold and stiff my body will lie.

The delicate grasp of an icy hold
against silk cushions, flesh will mold.

The soul's release shall come at last,
without a whisper or trumpet's blast.

In silence of a moonlit night,
body withers, soul takes flight.

Cry not for me beloved ones.
my soul is free, as the rising sun.

illustration by hermiona1988.deviantart.com

Angel of Twilight

My angel of the twilight;
with wings of dappled grey,
stepping from the shadows.

Your wings are ragged,
fluttering dejectedly
like forgotten wash.

Sweet angel of the twilight,
despondency is a shared
well of longing.

Wrap your arms around me,
lift me up, up, up
before we crash.

I walk the alleys,
I search the sewers,
for my veneration.

Bless me with putrid breath.
Lead me into temptation.
Deliver me to evil.

For I believe in
the all-encompassing spirits,
the holy communion of sinners.

The forgiveness of sins,
the resurrection of this frail body,
and life in lasting misery.

I descend into Hell,
with you, my twilight angel.
Amen.

The Escape Plan

My delicate earthly shell
encases a spirit wild and free.

A soul that longs to fly.
A heart that yearns to love.
A mind that wishes to excel.

Damn this transient fair flesh
that holds me back!

You wonder why I think of escape?
It holds me back, this earthly cloak.

I feel trapped.
I feel alone.
I feel, but I cannot do.

illustration by syntheticdreamer.deviantart.com

It Wasn't Your Job

Look at you.
Sitting there so calm.
An expression of mock humility.
Your eyes lowered.
Was it so I couldn't see
the fear and rage inside?

You raised your eyes again
there's that false repentance
I grew so used to.

You've added tears this time,
as if tears were still the
key to open my heart.
I changed the locks
while you were away.

Guess I didn't tell you.

I just stare blankly back at you.
I don't hate you.
I do hate being crushed into a box
that isn't my shape anymore.

You've raised your brow.
Does that mean you don't understand?
Does that mean you don't believe me?

Why does there have to be
a problem for me to have
the love I crave?

You said I was hard to love.
Am I impossible to love?

Love.

Do we know what that is?
Perhaps our hearts need
a trip to the library to
do a little research on
that vague emotion.

I was empty.

I thought you would fill me.
You couldn't.
It wasn't your responsibility,
but it still hurts.

Look at us.
Sitting here so calm.
While our world is pulled
out from under us.

illustration by acidDOTdica.deviantart.com

Mourning Dove

I know a mourning dove
nests in my soul.
Pale grey, its melancholy song
is a cooing plea for sanity.

It's always striving for peace,
but not yet holding that olive branch;
for peace has never been assured.

A boastful prospect perhaps,
though mournful tones sound
the accompaniment of the
lullaby of my soul's somber tune.

illustration by dgpc4ever.deviantart.com

Wake Up

I am nothing.

Perhaps my existence
is merely a dream
of someone the gods
wish to torment.

If that be true...

Wake up!

illustration by Pamela Borawski ~ druideye.deviantart.com

From the Edge

I stand at a crevasse
and backwards I fall.
Reaching up, up, up to you,
trying to grab your hand
as you stand right on the edge
staring down at me in horror.

I fall further and further down,
beaten upon snowy cheeks
by pelting pebbles and it's then
I realize as your hands are held out-
and as I move further from you-
that I did not stumble;
I was pushed by once loving hands
not reaching for me,
but pulling back after the push.

illustration by Pamela Borawski ~ druideye.deviantart.com

illustration by Pamela Borawski ~ druideye.deviantart.com

Whirlpool of Fate

The currents sweep me towards the whirlpool of fate.
Swimming upstream, against the torrential plan of my life.
Around and around thrashing wildly at the foam,
Charybdis summons and down, down I fall.

Spinning around in a whirlpool of fate.
Life flashes its colors, scenes of my life.
Desperate for a hand to hold on to,
I reach out for something that seemed to offer hope.

Swallowed down in the whirlpool of fate.
Clinging to the remaining shards of my life.
Hopeless and lonely, Scylla snaps at my hand.
Wounded, I alone, must face Fate's cruel plan.

Dark Parade

The mire of despondency
weighs us down considerably
yet the sun still shines
even behind grey clouds.

Ribbons of light shoot through the sky
catching the mist and dust
so that it sparkles like glitter;
like tickertape above my parade of sorrow.

The dark and desperate thoughts
march by on and on in my mind
no end in sight, repetitive as they
file one by one across my vision.

The pounding parade of agony
has become one with melancholia,
traveling side by side down
the blue avenue of desolation.

Fanfare in morbid tones herald
each passing memory with its
fluttering pennants marking the grief
of failed action and broken promises.

illustration by Pamela Borawski ~ druideye.deviantart.com

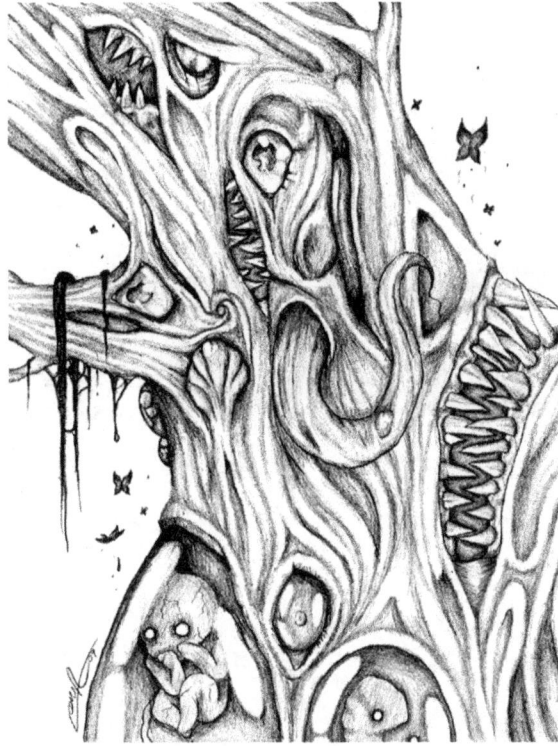

illustration by frozen-scumbag.deviantart.com

Bleeding Heart

The thorns of abuse
wrap around my heart
pricking its tender surface
and dripping its viscous vitae
like honey upon dry ground.

Tears wash over the flood
of bloody sorrow that
pines for a time when the
pain is no longer pulsing
along the entangling vines.

illustration by Pamela Borawski ~ druideye.deviantart.com

An Ocean of Sorrows

The tears stream down
only to be swallowed
by the pale flesh.

Salty sorrows,
the outward sign of
an inward destitute loneliness
and a frightened sadness.

Each drop but a
tiny flow of the ocean
that still ebbs within.

The Final Act

My flesh will wither,
and bones will whiten
for Death will find me
soon enough.

He has waited in the
wings since my debut,
and the act is nearly through.

The curtain call is almost done.
It's time to lay the roses for the
last time upon the planks at
final curtain fall.

illustration by Pamela Borawski ~ druideye.deviantart.com

Under My Skin

In silence, it screams.
In darkness, it blazes.
Creeping its way around
and around my mind
until there is no release.
In the night, it's awake.
In the daytime, it's sleeping
in my heart like some
slumbering giant trying
to explode through my
skin and pierce my
heart and mind.

illustration by dara-princess.deviantart.com

Tangled, Bloody Web

Translucent webs envelope my heart,
with passing time grow thicker.
Beating, beating, then retreating.
A gasp, as trembling mound
of flesh fights against the
sticky bonds that choke,
yet stay out of sight.

Weaving, weaving, then relieving
the body of a steady pulse.
Arachnophobic veins push harder,
as the network of invisible
threads grow stronger-
Pulling tighter, stifling breathing
as the hunter catches her prey.

Blood is pumping, muscles spasming
as the strands glimmer in the light!
Probing, probing, then we're hoping
that eradication of the problem
has given new life to choked heart.
Out she crawls, and circuit making,
'round and 'round the web is spun.

Creeping, creeping, heart now sleeping,
as a final tug is made.
Sticky strands of webbing covered
the heart and stops its beat.
Prey is captured, blood stops flowing,
now it hangs, dangling, by a string.

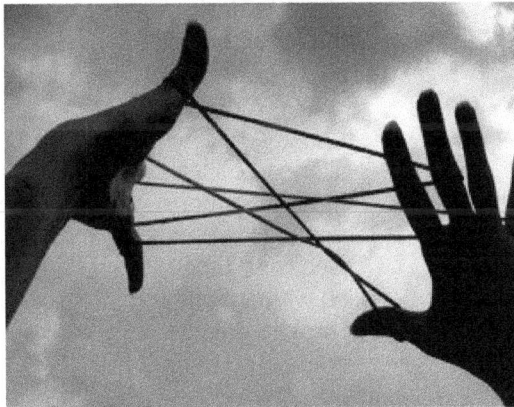

illustration by Regan Henley ~ popcorn-cob.deviantart.com

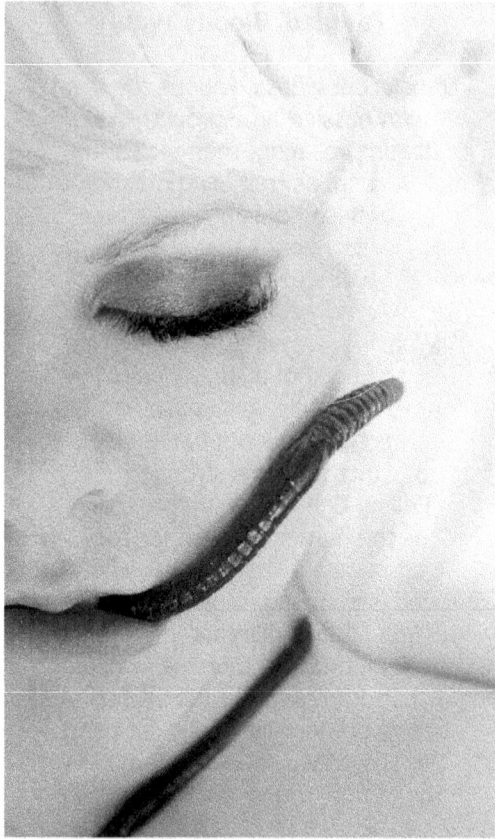
illustration by steamed-pepsi.deviantart.com

Fragile Vessel

Delight of worms,
crawling with filth.
Dust to dust,
the broken return
to the clay from which
he was formed.

Skin and bones
are nothing more
than molded vessels
used for a time-
filled with a lifetime
of broken dreams,
promises, screams,
loneliness, abandonment,
cruelty and sorrow.

Until the day
Thor's hammer falls
and the clay vessel shatters.
Our soul trickles free
of its captivity,
and back to the
ash and soil
this fleshly cloak
returns to be devoured.

Becoming one with earth again,
while our soul crosses
the bounds of eternity
to wander in the ethereality
of nothingness.

illustration by Pamela Borawski ~ druideye.deviantart.com

illustration by Regina Day ~ dead-poet.deviantart.com

Descendere

<u>Birth</u>
Tearing through flesh and bone
with a rage, a destiny-
Eyes closed, covered and nourished
by the dying body of a
woman who never wanted me.
You shouldn't have whispered
your secret fears. I heard them.
Now your torn body lies on a slab,
while I suck in the sweet air
and scream with preparation.

<u>Life</u>
As soon as we're born, we die.
Not right away, but gradually.
Humdrum mundane series of actions
that these insects call "living".
Utterly despise even a glance from them,
though it's the excuse - "They saw."
My hands grow grimy and sticky
exterminating the infestation.

<u>Death</u>
Pressure, intense pressure,
as my skin folds around me.
Breaking off into shards devoured
by maggots and roaches.
Another stone in a garden of memory,
down below the surface
something stirs, rage boils,
bubbling over-

A baby's first cry
echoes in the murky night.

illustration by natureofmind.deviantart.com

Self Portrait

Beautiful, unique,
quite insane.

Dark, deplorable,
inhumane.

Gentle, kind,
commendable.

Sinful, indecent,
a criminal.

Honest, patient,
unselfish.

Transgressor, trespasser,
generous.

Tender, protagonist,
diabolical.

Separated, desolated,
incorrigible.

Humble, amusing,
passionate.

Sullen, angry,
affectionate.

Frugal, sympathetic,
outrageous.

Depressed, hopeless,
courageous.

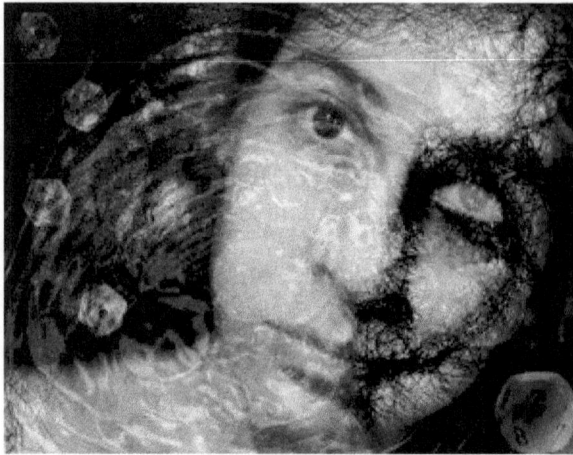

illustration by Andrea Schmoll ~ greenfaery.deviantart.com

Fickle Fates

The Fates are cruel bastards
if they so choose to be;
filling one life with torment
and one with prosperity.

I wonder, can I bribe them
with sweets and strawberry pie?
A lovely chocolate cake
and bon bons piled up high?

Oh, if they weren't so fickle,
as women seem to be...
I bet I could befriend them,
so they see what I want to see.

But alas, those Fates keep dishing
hope to her and not to me...
I guess I'm relegated
to a life of sheer misery.

The Ward

Soft, padded steps move around the bend
in tune to the gentle beeping of a heart.
Glow of the buzzing fluorescent lights
leaves an uncanny pallor upon wilted flesh.

Click. A door shuts; whispers flutter about.
Figures in white move slowly as they tend
to each moan, each tiny sputter of speech.
The lives of once strangers begin to enmesh.

From the sterile room the voices blend
as a scream drives pain into the known.
A broken body lays waiting for a mend
in a place of prayers for everyone's plights.

In the darkness a new angel will ascend,
signaling the loss of a history of fights.

illustration by Pamela Borawski ~ druideye.deviantart.com

Who Knows?

Who knows the worth of a true friend?
One who sticks around when all is at an end?

Bright lights on the horizon
catch my wandering eye.
I wonder if my ship's come in.
I whisper a prayer, "Will this one be a friend?"

Too easy, too easy,
my heart whispers to mind.
I succumb to pretty words,
soon our hearts entwine.

But shortly after, it's always the case,
drifting emptiness again I face.

illustration by Pamela Borawski ~ druideye.deviantart.com

This Prison Cell

These four walls, so stark and bare
cannot contain my spirit.
This broken body and broken mind
do nothing to hold back my soul
-though they try!

Beaten down like a bloody pulp,
like a worthless rag doll
thrown in the dump.

Good for nothing, in service to none,
yet my soul yearns for wings.
My mind wants to break free.

These mundane toxicological bars,
though they hold me tightly,
my freedom will come at a price.

Will the price of freedom be too high to pay
at the loss of something far too precious?

illustration by Sanja Gracej ~ niwaj.deviantart.com

The Truth of Justice

Justice is a foul desolation,
spitting promises that
rarely make good.

A desert wasteland of honor
among those who steal
our very souls.

Woe to those who walk through
the marble halls and
swear unholy truths.

Fear become of those whom
speak on high from profane altars,
their knife has drawn its fill.

Triangulation

Triangulation is the bane
of friendships young and old.
Such gossipy trysts of things mundane
oft lead to sorrows untold.

I tell you, "Please, don't say a word..."
Then empty out my soul;
and you turn 'round soon as you've heard
relaying my secrets you stole.

"So and so told me..." it starts out
as blinking the third party tells,
that secret entrusted without a doubt
to that friend you knew so well.

Triangulation strikes again;
its death to the honest person.
For if one will embrace the gossipy sin,
the friendship's failing is certain.

Tick Tock

D.T. 12.2008

illustration by blue-eyed-snidget.deviantart.com

Circling Hands

When these chains break,
hope flutters free.
Fixating on the future,
though the clock stopped-
Little bird, fly to me.

The hour has come,
the rain has gone.
Salty paths worn,
meandering,
vertically seduced by gravity.

Pulsing with the rhythm
of the heartbeat of twelve.
Half-past time to reset my mind,
a quarter of my life is over,
and any moment, the cock will crow.

Heartbreak

Your cusped words are like the sharpest blade,
they pierce my heart and they push me away.
My love, beloved! I beg you let me stay!
We'll work it out, this life that we have made.
My heart - your kiss, it was the smallest trade.
Your tender touch, I'll miss at break of day.
This my plea to you, we will find a way!
Don't send me out, alone, in bleak parade.

This thing we had, so good, gone forever.
What once had bloomed, now it's withered and dead.
My heart was full, now it's shrunk and severed.
I will not allow sad despair and dread,
to bring me down; whispering "no, never".
Her face, so near! - Now I'm alone in bed.

illustration by Regan Henley ~ popcorn-cob.deviantart.com

Cure My Disease

The seed of darkness lies buried
in a hidden place in my heart.

Merely lying in recession
awaiting a spark, a melancholy night.

Fertilized by the shadows of doom,
tiny tendrils snake out and
slowly begin to pierce the dainty
shell of hope which surrounded
the fragile heart, and wounded soul.

Like a cancerous growth extending
and gripping tighter, abhorring light,
it rescinds its mantra to stay down.

The cure for the disease is not
found in broken relationships
struggling to be maintained.

The cure for the plague is not
smiling, grabbing life by the horns
and surviving; keeping your chin up.

No, the darkness is only held
in check by a handful of colorful capsules,
which, like knights against a dragon foe,
fight the choking vines of darkness
forcing it back into its secret lair -

Where it waits and procreates,
awaiting a spark, a melancholy night.

In a hidden place within my heart,
the seed of darkness still lies buried.

illustration by Regina Day ~ dead-poet.deviantart.com

Two Voices

There are two voices within my head,
one builds me up,
one tears me down.

The negative voice screams so loud,
saying I'm nothing.
saying I'm nothing.

Lies bespoke so very long ago,
seem to be true,
bury deep within.

Burrowing within every emotion, it
speaks without care,
feelings aren't spared.

The positive voice from two that I love
whisper so soft,
barely is heard.

Overpowered again, voice one says,
you're nothing, understand?
You are nothing.

And you'll never amount to anything,
you're a failure,
a waste of air.

Bryllwen's Lament

I walk a path of dark despair,
all those I see, you should beware.
My fate is sealed, I cannot lie.
care for my soul if you so dare.

My fate is sealed, this is the truth.
I have become cold and aloof.
The circumstances of my life,
confuse me now, I have no proof.

The circumstances make me think,
and push me towards the very brink.
So hard for me to even breathe,
as deep in mire I slowly sink.

So hard for me to stay my mind.
Lucidity is hard to find.
I am so near the breaking point,
mind, heart and soul cannot align.

I am so near insanity,
Death calls to me and makes his plea.
All that I loved has gone away,
I fear for my stability.

All that I loved has turned to dust,
I blame it all on induced lust.

That which I was, I will n'er be,
the guilt and pain has shattered me.

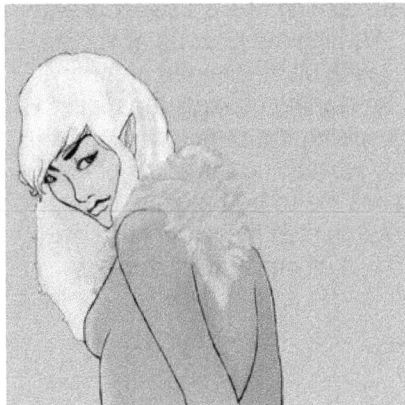

illustration by number89.deviantart.com

illustration by shane-01.deviantart.com

Insane Stupidity

Standing on the brink of insanity,
I raise my voice and fists toward eternity.
Screaming at life's sweet brevity.
Turning my nose up at society,
with all its planned propriety.
Its leaning towards the majority.
Despising the search for popularity.
My weakening threshold of civility,
beckons me to become one of depravity.
Astounded by all the false piety,
it all ends up as stupidity.

For the One I Lost

His voice still haunts me
in the recesses of my mind,
where no matter how I try
I cannot escape
the smile,
the soft touch,
the laughter,
the love.

I was barely alive then
and he was my messiah.
My stronghold in trouble.
My strong arms
to hold me,
to cry with,
to lean upon,
to love.

I opened a box not long ago
and inside were your letters.
Long, edification in wood and ink.
We should have built upon it,
held tight to it,
relied on it.

But we denied it.

His voice still haunts
the recesses of my mind,
and a whisper is buried
the whisper, "still time" .

illustration by Pamela Borawski ~ druideye.deviantart.com

No Trespassing

A dilapidated soul
rotted, falling apart,
empty for years,
vacated by necessity.
The residents are only those things
that come out in the dark of the night.
"No Trespassing" hung on the door.
Only those seeking malice
walk through into its dark space.

illustration by Daniella Koontz ~ doubtful-della.deviantart.com

Same Difference

Garb yourself in ebon
to show the state of your heart.
Maybe it's a form of hiding
yet residing in plain sight.

Hints of happiness mar the visage.
Pushed aside, make room for
the masochistic enamored one;
dwelling beneath pale skin and ruby, unsmiling lips.

Torture your body, make it hurt...
physical pain drowns out inner pain,
at least for a brief respite in time.

Contort the beauty of a past life.
The standard has changed.
Has it lowered or raised?

The opinion of the mass herds
matter not at all.

Stand out, be different,
yet in your difference
you have become
the same.

Lavender

I'm breaking little by little,
though you can't see me
falling apart.

I'm afraid of being seen
for who I really am.

I'm hiding behind a dream,
pretending I'm alright.

Smiles hide the confusion,
laughter hides the tears.

One day I'll crash and break
into so many pieces
they will never be recovered.

I'll leave behind
some words,
some memories.

As I break into final pieces,
the world will smell of
lavender.

Portrait of my Grief

It's an emptiness so deep within
you can't seem to reach the bottom.

The whisper in the night
and no one's there.

It's when your happiness is
twinged with sorrow for
there is something missing
from the joyous occasion.

It's sitting alone on a porch swing,
remembering a porch swing
that saw many years of use.

It's a rain tree in the front yard
you'll never climb again.

Certain words that will never
sound in your ear again
like "Punkin," and "My granddaughter."

An inner anguishing that
mere tears will not quench.

It's a visit where you stand above
and look down instead of
standing beside and looking up.

It's the thought of going to Disney
without him...and declining.
Its loneliness and sadness
and longing all in one.

Its pain so great it hurts to think,
so great you think you'll never be healed.

It's never reaching the bottom
of an emptiness that's deep within.

The End

Trembling on the verge of a new day.
Teetering on the edge of a new way.

My foundation begins to crumble
and I begin to tumble.
Grasping for anything...
Reaching for everything...

If only I could bend my will,
It's as though the gods know my Achilles heel.
Alone, head over heels I fall.
Exhilaration! Beaten about like a rag doll.

My tenacious fortitude fails,
as towards the bottom my body sails.
It will soon be over, it will soon be through,
there's nothing left to say or do.

I expect my body will shatter.
It's not like I ever mattered.
Nightshade in a garden of light,
nothing I did ever turned out right.

The rocks at the bottom call out my name,
"Pamela!" they shout, "Is ugly and plain!
Your death will bring so many glee,
your sorry life wasn't meant to be!"

Dashed upon the angry rocks,
like my hopes, a precarious lot.
Broken body with broken dreams,
my life plays out its final scene.

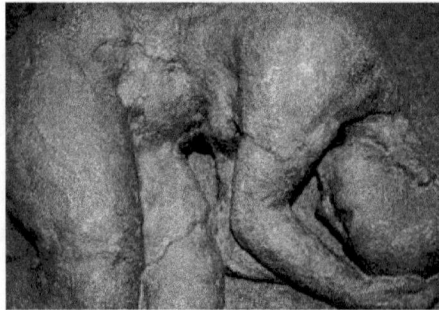

illustration by Pamela Borawski ~ druideye.deviantart.com

104